C000165381

Jeremy Harte has been investigating Dorset folklore for sixteen years, since the days when he grew up in Abbotsbury. After graduating from Cambridge, he worked in the archaeological section of the Dorset County Museum in Dorchester before training as a curator. At present he runs the Bourne Hall Museum at Ewell in Surrey. Jeremy has written books on folklore, industrial archaeology and local history.

Following page
The Cerne Giant, Cerne Abbas. The Giant is Dorset's most enigmatic figure, and to this day, a source of legend, folklore, speculation and controversy.

DISCOVER DORSET

LEGENDS

JEREMY HARTE

THE DOVECOTE PRESS

An engraving of the Agglestone before it toppled.

First published in 1998 by The Dovecote Press Ltd
Stanbridge, Wimborne, Dorset BH21 4JD

ISBN 1 874336 56 3

Series designed by Humphrey Stone

Typeset in Sabon by The Typesetting Bureau
Wimborne, Dorset
Printed and bound by Baskerville Press, Salisbury, Wiltshire

A CIP catalogue record for this book is available
from the British Library

1 3 5 7 9 8 6 4 2

CONTENTS

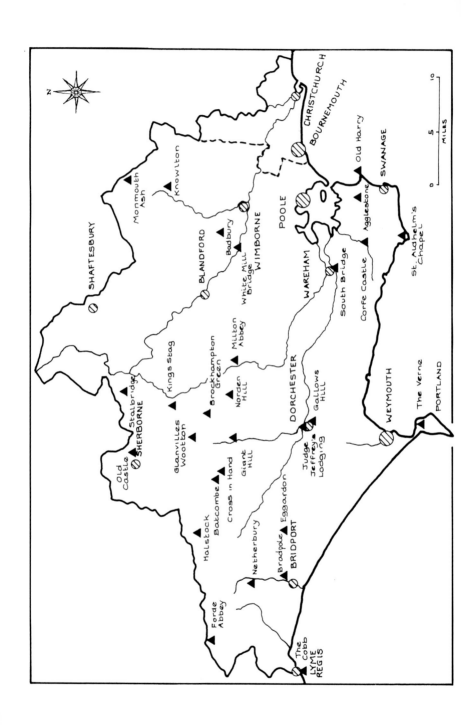

INTRODUCTION

When the old people had something worth saying, they said it in a story. It is an old art, doubtless much older than the written traditions which have preserved it, and these themselves go back a thousand years. When the authentic voice of Dorset people is first recorded, in Latin and Old English, they are already looking back to the heroic days of the past. The tradition carries on, swelling through time, from monastic chronicles through faded broadsheets to the cramped notepads of folklorists. This is a book of the legends which have been told about Dorset's past.

These stories have been carved out of the flotsam of history. They contain everything that real history doesn't – simple causes, clear-cut right and wrong, and the intervention of God when things go astray. Do remember: it didn't necessarily happen this way, if it ever happened at all.

Not that legends are always (factually) wrong. A tradition is a story handed down, whether or not that story was real. Three men feature in stories at Milton Abbey, and each tale matches up with truth in a different way. Lord Milton was never really eaten by lice, an un-likely but spine-tingling fate. Though Athelstan certainly won a great battle, it was in another part of the country altogether and the intervention of saints on the day is doubted by historians. But young John Tregonwell really did fall from the battlements of Milton Abbey and live – and he was not the only one. Girls went over cliffs and survived at a dozen spots from Bristol to Berne, whenever hooped skirts were in fashion. They appear in the newspapers, but have a mythic ring for all that. Each one, picking herself up off the ground, must have had the strange feeling of being more than half a legend.

It is the task of stories to take all the confusing detail of real life, and smooth it into simpler, grander patterns. Though almost every-one in this book did live and die in Dorset, it is not their individual features that matter any longer: behind them, large and indistinct as shadows cast by the firelight, are their images as the heroes and villains of legend. When it comes to stories, time and space cease to matter. Wherever there are great rocks, there will be a giant who hurled them about; he is first heard of in ancient Greece, he has left his mark on lands from Ireland to Japan, and we know of him at Cheselbourne.

Long before Jones the lawyer met his fiery end at Lyme Regis, the souls of the wicked were seen by pious hermits being tossed into Etna and Stromboli. St. Aldhelm's ride on the demon steed is the same story that they tell in the Border country about the wizard Michael Scot. The gruesome anecdote of the hanged man and the bowl of soup is told in Shrewsbury almost word for word as they relate it in Dorchester, and, of course, the inhabitants of both towns think that it really happened in their own locality. It is just the same when the people of Fishguard lay claim to the trick of women soldiers in red coats, not thinking that at least three Dorset communities have made the story their own.

But although legends leapfrog so easily from place to place they are, paradoxically, rooted in the soil wherever they belong. Almost every narrative in this book can be pinpointed, not to a district or village, but to the landmark of the story itself – the diabolical Agglestone, the Monmouth Ash, St. Edward's Well, all of these remain to bear witness. Sometimes it was the monument which came first, and the story simply grew on it like lichen. Many tales of medieval knights have come about this way, as a well-meaning verger or a cleaning lady tries to make sense of a weathered effigy.

Of course the old storytellers knew more than these tales of heroism in days gone by. They could tell of witchcraft and of prophecies, they knew anecdotes about village characters, they could interpret bizarre customs and local nicknames. The collective memory of the village held charms, songs, riddles and jokes: most of all, there were and are the ghost stories. A full survey of the Dorset narrative tradition would be more than half made up out of ghosts, especially now that the fairies are gone and witchcraft carries so little weight. I have kept the ghosts at bay in this book, in case they took it over completely, though many of the stories here tell of similar themes – bravery in the face of danger, tragic death, and the mysterious interference of the supernatural in human affairs.

All the stories here have been retold. Had the words of the original storytellers been preserved, it would have been a shame to lose them: but written accounts are rarely more than notes taken by those who listened, often without sympathy. They are no more the real thing than a dried insect on a pin is the butterfly in the meadow. I have not broken faith with the stories by adding incidents or changing emphasis – what is here, give or take a little local colour, is the original. (Readers who want to find the actual sources can consult the annotated copies of this book which have been left at the Dorset County Museum and Dorchester Library).

Sometimes there has been a little tucking and piecing, when a story carried on in a second account where the first left off. In the martyrdom of St. Edward, I followed William of Malmesbury's chronicle as far as the king's death, and then switched to Brompton's because he had more to say about the miracles that happened at Corfe. Not that either author was in a position to know what really happened in 979: in fact, with the benefit of hindsight, we can see that they took it for granted that Aelfthryth was a wicked stepmother, which is not true. I have echoed the author of the *Vita Oswaldi*, for whom the young Edward was an image of Christ, but it is hard to know what other hints and ambiguities are in the original Latin. When the queen offers him a cup of wine, is it an image from the pagan epic tradition, or are we to remember the martyr's cup of Matthew 20:23?

A thousand years later, the meanings of this story are still alive, still debated. At Brookwood in Surrey, the Russian monks kneel before Edward's shrine because he is an Orthodox saint. At Shaftesbury, people campaign furiously for its return because he is a Wessex king. A world in which people will go to law over a casket of old bones is clearly one in which the mythical is very much alive.

Legends articulate what we often feel, but cannot directly say. The stories from Portland are not just about Vikings and Cavaliers who died long ago; they are also a stubborn defence of the Island as its people would like it to be – self-sufficient, unsubdued, with a trick to meet every threat from that other world across the Chesil Bank. The tale of the women who killed the invaders has come a long way – it was the story of the Danaides in Homer's day, and who knows what community it was told of before then? Here and now, set against the unforgiving background of Portland stone, it is an emblem of secret resistance.

A whole book could be written, too, about what tradition tells us of Dorset's relationship with the sea. Monsters and treasure come up out of the sea: so do the harvests of fish, more reliable than those of the land, and so does smuggled brandy. Sometimes strange men are thrown up by the sea – Swanage Spaniards, Symondsbury Danes. Sometimes the sea takes men back again, a whole ship's crew at once, only those who can hear the voice of prophecy being saved.

Although traditions of the supernatural are growing apace, it seems that the age of the full-blooded legend is dead. The myth-history of Dorset comes to an end with scattered stories from the Napoleonic era, and no-one has been tempted to add to it. As long as tradition really counted, while it had the force of common law, it could sum up what people thought about the past. Now it has been driven out by written facts: indeed, the last episodes in traditional history are about criminals, people who keep their lives secret and write nothing down. Nowadays nobody is tempted to tell heroic stories about, for instance, the two World Wars. The facts can be looked up in a book, if need be. But people still tell stories about ghosts – for where is the book that can tell you the truth about ghosts? Instead of tales about a legendary past, we are assailed by rumours about mysteries here and now. The giants and heroes have gone, and in their place we glimpse the UFOs of Poole Harbour, and that marvellous beast the Weymouth Veasta – the half-real creatures of a mythical present.

GIANTS AND THE DEVIL

A legend, in the original sense of the word, is a saint's life. Over the years, chroniclers acquired the habit of saying much about the lives of saints that was not strictly true – for instance, that St. Augustine passed through Dorset early in his missionary career, that he was stopped in his tracks by a vision of the divine splendour, and that in his fierce ecstasy he cried *'Cerno Hel'*, which is dog-Latin and Hebrew for 'I see God'. So impressed were the locals by the stranger's cry that they renamed the village after the unfamiliar words, and Cerne it has been ever since.

Now it is true that Cerne is really named after the river that flows through its chalkland valley, just as it is true that Augustine never came here – in fact, that the whole story is the invention of a pious hack, one Goscelin, who was invited to Cerne Abbey in 1100 to improve its pedigree by a bit of creative writing. But I don't think that Goscelin would have been in the least taken back by accusations of inventiveness.

'What!' he would have said. 'Do you really want to be bothered with lists of dead abbots, when I can offer holy words about the Apostle of the English? – how he crossed the dry Downs to where shepherds sat gasping in the shade of a thorn tree, and came amongst them like an angel, crying "Choose your liquor! Wine or water?" '

'Water,' they said, for they knew the virtue of temperance.

'Well spoken,' said the saint, 'for if it had been wine you wished for, I should have given you enough for a day: but the water which I give you will last until the end of the world.'

And he struck the ground with his staff, and obedient to the touch of the saint it trembled and bubbled up a spring of living water, which folk call St. Augustine's Well – and to this day everyone who visits the place can go and drink from it, in a little dip round the back of the abbey.

St. Augustine's Well, Cerne Abbas, originally covered by a medieval chapel.

'And if that's not a spiritually edifying story,' says Goscelin, 'I don't know what is. Don't talk to me about facts. Nobody ever got saved by facts.'

What Goscelin would have thought of the Cerne Giant is anybody's guess, and there are certain sullen antiquarians who think that he never had the opportunity, since the Giant was carved out of the chalk five hundred years after the Norman monk was laid in his grave. But there is more to the Giant than facts. At night, when the wrangling of archaeologists and historians is hushed in sleep, he comes down off the hill to quench his day-long thirst in the millstream. This happens every time he hears the church clock strike midnight – and those who claim that a chalk figure cannot hear have, perhaps, missed the point.

In his younger days, the Giant used to get around a lot more than this. Cudgel-play was the great game then – any lad might join in once he held a club in one hand, had padded the other with enough wadding to ward off blows, and was prepared to hammer away at his opponent till the blood flowed onto the sticky boards of the ring.

The Kevels Inn, up by Middlemarsh, used to be the great place for this, when Dorset was able to take on the teams of Somerset and Wiltshire and send them both home with broken heads. The smell of the dark blood would come to the nostrils of the Giant – for he can smell, as well as hear – and he would rise from off the hill. People heard him bellow, 'Fee fi fo fum', after the manner of giants, as he stalked to the booths around the inn. It wouldn't have been possible for him to join in, of course, but he made an unanswerable referee – what they used to call a stickler: we still speak of as 'a stickler for fair play'.

Later on he went to the bad, and roamed between Dorchester and the Blackmore Vale killing and devouring. At last Cerne folk had had enough, and they hatched a plan. Crowded indoors, they heard the great footsteps pulverising the Dorchester road – travellers can see the pits to this day, each one with a clump of trees growing in it. They felt the shock as the Giant swung his frying pan down on top of the hill, leaving a round scar for all the world like the remains of an ancient earthwork. Then, peeping through cracks in the doors, they saw him stretch his great length out on the hill for a nap in the afternoon sunlight. Quietly, going from house to house, they brought out lengths of ships' cable and iron pegs; then streaming up to the hill they criss-crossed the rope over his sleeping form and tamped it down until it formed a web from which not even a titan's strength could stir an inch. Even the club was strapped down. As the Giant woke and felt himself bound, the shepherd boy who had suffered most at his hands stepped up and killed him. Then, by way of a memorial, all the people dug a trench around his vast form, so that the image would remind future generations of the danger from which they had been spared.

The rampages of giants were terrible in those ancient days. Up in the Blackmore Vale, at the hamlet of Brockhampton Green, they have left another memorial. It is a stone, lying by the roadside. This was the stratagem hit on by the people of Buckland Newton and district when their flocks and children were being ravaged by a monster – one who, like his brother at Cerne, liked to lie down on a hillside and sleep off his grisly dinner. All the people crept together, found the largest stone they could, and commenced rolling it up to the crest of the hill. One more heave and it would reach the top, to career wildly down the slope and flatten their old enemy as it went. Unfortunately, shortly before reaching Brockhampton Green they ran out of puff and gave the whole thing up as a bad job. The giant of Buckland lived to a ripe old age, after all.

Others say that it was the giant who dropped the stone, or maybe he threw it to its present position. Hurling the quoit, or putting the stone, was a favourite manly pastime in those days, and one well suited to the limited intellect of the giants. They would challenge each other to great contests in it; when two giants met on Norden Hill by Melcombe Horsey, one challenged the other to a game, and pointed out Hanging Hill a mile away as the target. The sandstone boulder which he hurled towards it landed a thousand yards off in the valley – a tidy throw. Then the other giant ripped up a rock to show what *he* could do, and sent it soaring through the air, but alas! the throw fell short – a couple of yards behind the first one. Grief and rage coursed across the features of the great oaf until, from mere frustration, his heart broke and he crashed lifeless to the ground. His fellow giants carried him down to the valley and buried him beside the fatal stones in a great mound, which is still called the Giant's Grave.

The long burial mounds of the chalk hills are not the only evidence of this vanished race. Maiden Castle, the Verne on Portland, and all the other earthworks so confidently identified by archaeologists as hillforts were in fact the fortified homesteads of giants. The great ramparts, still impressive to this day, are a witness to what can be done with brute strength – in fact the main difficulty was to get tools which would suit the colossal size of the workmen.

When two giants were digging out Spetisbury Rings and Badbury Rings, there was only one pick and one shovel to hand, so they had to go shares; one would hack away with the pick breaking up the ditches, then stroll over five miles to where his colleague had been shovelling up the ramparts, and swap tools; and so they carried on until the work was finished. For a lot of digging went on in those early days.

The massive earthwork which parts Dorset from Wiltshire, known as Bokerley Dyke, has also been called Grim's Ditch. Why Grim

The sarsen stone on the Giant's Grave, between Cheselbourne and Binghams Melcombe.

An aerial view of Chesil Beach and the Fleet, with Portland in the distance.

should have dug it, or who he was – whether giant, hero, or spirit – are things now forgotten, though some have thought he was the Devil. Certainly the Devil was busy with mattock and spade elsewhere, his works including the Roman Road which runs from Dorchester towards the hillfort at Eggardon. Satanic power, as well as brute strength, must have been needed here, since the job was finished in a single night. In the same way, the Chesil Bank – all the way from Weymouth to West Bay – appeared in a single night. When people went to bed, Portland was still an island: when they set out to work in the morning, the sunlight glittered on the wet stones of a nine-mile causeway linking it to the mainland.

The Devil was always interfering with the landscape: seafarers

The Agglestone, a natural conglomerate block on Studland Heath.

seem to have been the particular butt of his malice. He used to perch on the Needles, far off on the other side of the Solent, waiting for the shipping to go down. Once he dozed off, and woke with a start to see the setting moon silhouetted westward behind the battlements of Corfe Castle. The tranquil beauty of the sight would have melted a softer heart, but it could only madden the fiend. Chattering with rage he tore off his night-cap (it was a chilly night) and hurled it at the offending towers. Fortunately the Devil's night-cap fell short of its target, and landing on the Island of Purbeck it turned into a stone outcrop – the Agglestone of Studland Heath. It is a curious witness to the Devil's markmanship, but the Agglestone does indeed lie in a direct line between Corfe Castle and the Needles.

The Devil must have had a soft spot for Studland, after all, because Old Harry, the chalk pinnacle below the cliffs there, is named after him. There was an Old Harry's Wife, too, but she went down before the blast of a storm a hundred years ago, since when he has been a widower. Other pinnacles nearby are his daughter, and their haystack. The adjoining stretch of cliff is Old Nick's Ground, and the caves underneath are the Devil's Den. It's a queer thing about these caves – they are always warm. Fishermen used to shelter there after setting lobster pots on a November morning, to get the frost out of their bones before they started homeward. The cliffs were seared by the fires of hell when the Devil was in residence, and they can never quite forget the experience.

It was while he was hunched up in one of these caves that the Devil conceived another of his malicious plans – this time it was the destruction of Stonehenge. Churches and cathedrals were as yet unknown, but the Purbeck stone industry was in full swing, and the quarries were full of half-worked blocks and scants. Unfurling his black wings, the fiend wrenched off a mass of stone from the workface and flew ominously north – but he had misjudged his strength and he had to drop his burden on the bare heath. Back he went, and picked up a more modest block; this time he made it as far as Wimborne, where a sudden blast of wind threw him off balance, and the stone splashed down into the River Allen. People who lean over the bridge on summer days can still see it when the water is clear. A third visit to the Kimmeridge quarries, and the Devil was flying back optimistically to Wiltshire with a slender length of stone. At last Stonehenge was in site and he flapped down, scattering the white-robed Druids, and poised the block to throw . . . but it slipped from his claws just outside the circle. There it stands embedded in the ground – they call it the Heel Stone. The Devil went home in disgust.

The Devil had it pretty much his own way in those pagan days. It was later on, when holy men began to be thicker on the ground, that things became uncomfortable for the prince of this world. On one occasion he was up to no good in the Marshwood Vale, having stupidly failed to notice that Forde Abbey had been built since his last visit. The abbot caught him at it, there was a brief altercation, and

Forde Abbey, which after the Dissolution of the Monasteries was remodelled as the seat of the Prideaux family.

Satan was evicted from the monastery grounds with a kick up the rear. It must have been some kick, because he sailed through the air to land by a clump of trees on the nearest hill, bounced up and came to earth at a second clump, and then sailed through the air a third time to land at Birdsmoorgate. The abbot's jurisdiction ended there and he thought no more about it – besides, in those days, before the government started messing about with county boundaries, Forde was in Devon and Birdsmoorgate was the Dorset boundary. Dorset people say that the Devil carried on bouncing from one clump of trees to another (they are all called the Devil's Jumps) until he splashed into the sea at West Bay. Devon folk are not so sure.

SAINTS AND MIRACLES

The Devil's power was as nothing when confronted with the influences of the saints. Some of them, like St Aldhelm, were even prepared to put him to undignified uses. There was a time, in the early years of Aldhelm's ministry among the West Saxons, when his fame came to the ears of the Pope, and he was invited to Rome. Quite an honour, but unfortunately the messenger was held up crossing the Channel, and by the time he rode breathless and flustered into the bishop's palace at Sherborne, there were only two days left before the proposed date of meeting. Who could pass through seas and mountains and barbarians in so short a time?

'Leave it to me,' said the saint, as he saddled and bridled a passing fiend. 'Fast or slow?' he said, and the evil spirit cried, 'I am as swift as the bird in the air!'

'Tsk, tsk', went St. Aldhelm, letting him go and reaching for another one. 'Fast or slow?'

'I am as swift as an arrow from a warrior's bow!' exulted the second, but that wouldn't do either.

The third spirit said, 'I am as swift as a wise man's thought,' and he was got ready for the journey. Aldhelm packed lightly, sprung onto his uncanny steed, and thought of the great dome of St. Peters. Next moment, his foot was grazing against the cross on its roof. He steered his mount down to earth, where it stood in the form of a great black horse, looking down on the crowd who had come streaming out into the square to see such a wonder. The saint dismounted, threw the reins to a servant, and told him to take good care of his mount.

'Does he need feeding, master?' said the ostler.

'Oh yes,' said Aldhelm. 'About a bucket of live coals should do.'

This caused quite a stir, and the Pope persuaded Aldhelm to use more orthodox means of transport thereafter, so that the next time he was called to Rome he had to wait for a ship like everyone else. In those days they sailed from Wareham, and the winds happened to be contrary, so that St. Aldhelm found himself with time on his hands. Roaming through the neighbouring heath, and finding how ignorant the furzecroppers were in matters of religion, he set to and built them a church. He laid its walls singlehanded with the dark ironstone of the heath, and roofed it with wooden shingles. He had just consecrated the church and made it fit for the celebration of the holy mysteries when the winds changed, and he had to take sail. Discreditably, the men of Arne failed to take care of the saint's handiwork, and after a few years the shingles got loose and the whole roof blew off in a winter gale. But though men had forgotten to honour the saint, the weather knew better. Each time it rained, the drops were careful to swerve right or left rather than profane the holy place, and so the ruined chapel remained as dry as if the roof was still above it. It was very convenient. People got into the habit of sheltering there during a downpour, and shepherds made for it with their drenched flocks, until at last the battered walls were no more than a sheepfold.

In the end Dorset was won over to Christian ways, but it was a slow business. In Halstock, within sight of the towers of Sherborne Abbey, a young girl called Juthware was converted to the new teachings and listened eagerly, night after night, to the news brought by holy men as they rested awhile on the long tramp to Glastonbury. Soon her house became a hostel for pilgrims, who filled it night and day with the praise of God, and ate up most of what was in the larder. This went down badly with Juthware's stepmother, a woman who knew the value of money. Her heart hardened, and at length she thought of a plan. During one of their late-night mother-daughter chats, Juthware had confided that she was suffering from pains in the chest; now her stepmother took her aside and said she had found the perfect cure. It was cream cheese, to be rubbed on liberally as an ointment. Juthware stammered her thanks, and took a pot up to her room.

Next day the stepmother waited for the son of the house to come home, and confronted him on the theshold, arms folded. Did he know his sister was pregnant? That was what came of letting her stay up all night with those so-called pilgrims, and it was going to have to

The centre of Halstock, where until recently St Juthware's death was commemorated by a pub called The Quiet Woman.

stop. The lad was taken aback, and muttered something about needing a bit more proof.

'Proof?' she said, grabbing a vest from the washing basket, 'here's proof enough – smell this.'

Sure enough, there was a milky smell on the garment, where some of the cream cheese had rubbed off, and that was enough to persuade the gullible lad that his family honour had been defiled. He picked up a sword and stormed off to the neighbouring hill, where Juthware sat innocently keeping watch over the sheep. With one sweeping blow he hacked right through her neck. A little blood trickled down: and then, silently, she picked up her head and walked with it to Halstock church. There Juthware placed her head on the altar, from which it gazed in mute rebuke at her stunned relatives until, as they knelt in prayer, the eyes slowly closed. Over on the other side of the chancel her body swayed and fell, and so she died.

Many years later, body and head were fetched away together to be held in honour at Sherborne Abbey: but even so, Halstock has not forgotten its holy daughter (see front cover illustration). The hill where she died is still known as Judith, and until its closure her portrait appeared on the sign of the village pub, though they called it The Quiet Woman.

Won over by the holy deeds of the saints, Dorset people began to build their own churches, but they had some confused ideas about how to do it. Villagers in Bradpole argued passionately over a place for the new faith, and eventually hit on a site next to their old orchard, because if there had been any religion in the west of Dorset before then, it was cider. Apple trees flourished in every valley between Bridport and Forde, and come springtime the villages were hidden under a frothy veil of white blossom. Tom Putts, Poor Mans Profits. . . everyone had their favourite variety, but as far as Bradpole people were concerned they were just wasting their time. The Bradpole Bitterseal was the only cider apple worth bothering about, and every garden in the village had its own, most of them grafted from one venerable tree that grew below the hill. It seemed somehow fitting to put the new religion in there too, and as the first churchwardens strolled down to inspect the site, their talk was more of April frosts and caterpillars than of prayer and good works. As they came nearer, a terrible sight met their eyes. Their stroll quickening to a run, they raced to grab the two villains who had just been about to lay an axe to the roots of the old tree. On closer inspection the villains turned out to be the very same workmen hired for the new building, who were indignant about being interrupted in their

Holy Trinity, Bradpole, built in 1845 to replace the medieval church.

labours. They had just been about to clear the site for the church – here were the footings for the tower, and there would be the chancel, just where that old tree stood in the way, standing due east. 'Hang due east!' cried the churchwardens, 'build your chancel anywhere you like, so long as it does not disturb our tree.' The workmen shrugged their shoulders, and complied. Many years have passed since then; rot and winter storms have long since done for the old tree, and even the stone church has been rebuilt, but it still retains the twist which was given it to avoid the Bradpole Bitterseal.

Building a church was never easy, no matter how carefully the site might be chosen. At East Chelborough the people of the village could not afford to hire professional stonemasons, so they agreed to work together and do the building themselves. A field beside the road was set apart to be consecrated ground, and the first day's work went well enough. There was a holiday atmosphere to the task, and at the end of the day everyone was proud to see the first course of new stones marking the outline of the church. When daylight faded they split up into twos and threes to go home, boasting cheerfully of what would be done next morning. The sky grew dark, and a lonely moon rose above Castle Hill, the ancient earthwork that lay above the village. There were banks and ditches here, crumbling into ruin: they had been abandoned centuries ago, but Castle Hill was not uninhabited. The villagers knew that it was the home of fairies, and avoided it whenever they could. Now, however, as the moonlight shone on the grassy slopes, the people of the night came pouring angrily down the hill, buzzing like a swarm of bees when some thoughtless boy has kicked their hive. They had no love for priests or churches, and the sight of the grey outlines of masonry seemed to rouse them to frenzy. All at once a cluster of hunched figures squatted around each stone, and suddenly they sprang up, bearing the stubborn weight as if it were thistledown, and flew off through the night with it. A mile away, in the neighbouring hamlet of Lewcombe, their course was blocked by running water, and they halted in a plot of overgrown meadow and dropped the unwelcome stones one by one, leaving the outline of the church plotted out in the long grass just as it had been before. Then they turned in mid-air and, like a flash of lightning, shot back to the green darkness within Castle Hill.

The remains of the medieval motte and bailey castle on
Castle Hill at Chelborough.

Next morning Chelborough people were up with the sun, spitting on their hands and ready to carry on with the great work. But when they came to the field by the road, there was nothing left of yesterday's achievement – nothing at all. The grass quivered in the wind, unbroken, where the trenches had been surveyed and dug with such effort before. And coming up the road, almost speechless with rage, were the farmers of Lewcombe, wanting to know what Chelborough folk meant by dumping great heaps of stone down in their meadows.

At last a horse and cart were sent down to Lewcombe to retrieve the wandering masonry, while people worked to prepare the site again. It was a hot day, and they sweated in the sunshine as a new outline was hacked out on the ground and trenches were dug afresh. At last in the cool of the evening they left for home, one or two villagers casting nervous glances over their shoulders. They might as well not have bothered. As soon as darkness prevailed, the glistening horde swept down again from Castle Hill, and carried the stones back off to the meadow at Lewcombe. When the villagers of Cheselborne returned to the scene of their failed hopes on the third day, they were hardly surprised to find it as bare as before. Fetching back the stones, they made some half-hearted attempts to lay out the proposed building, but when on the morning of the next day the

East Chelborough church, built at Lewcombe in the early sixteenth century.

stonework was found back at the lower site, they gave in and built the church in the secluded quiet of Lewcombe meadows.

It is hard to get the better of spirits, but it can be done. Portland used to be thick with a kind of fairies called the pexies, who slipped out at night to dance among the fields in the barren landscape. The arable land here was divided up into strips, with long thin balks of grass laid out to connect them, and on moonlit nights the pexies could be seen as they raced along these, looking for places where they might hold their revels. Wherever they danced, they left behind them a dark green circle in the grass – a fairy ring. The supernatural origin of these was proved by their use in magic. If you made a wish, and then danced three times round the circle as the pexies had done, you would receive whatever you wanted within a year; and if you were bold enough to run around one of these rings nine times, without ever drawing breath, a pexy would appear to you bringing something good.

Not all encounters with the fairy kingdom were so fortunate.

Among the pexies there was one who took no part in the joyful dancing on the grassy balks, but wandered alone through the fields, carrying a light with him: because of this, people called him Jack o' Lantern. On cloudy nights, when the shapes of paths and hedges had become indistinct, Jack would go bobbing up and down with his eerie light, which shone brightly without casting a shadow, and seemed to burn without warmth. Many an unwary traveller, caught far from home after nightfall, saw the light and took it for something more familiar; perhaps the welcoming gleam of fire in a house, or a real lantern held by another wanderer in the night who could show him the way back to the main path. So he would strike out across the fields towards it, stumbling across the rocky waste of the quarries. As he grew closer, the light moved – just a little – and he stepped hastily after it, tearing his clothes on the furze that grows everywhere on the high ground. Before he could gain on it, the light had moved again, and so the chase went on: until at last the light stopped, and the traveller ran towards it, angry and frightened. But it had stopped at the cliff's edge. The man scrabbled and clutched at the ground sloping under him, and as he screamed in his long fall down, the light hovered cold and motionless above the terrifying gap. Jack o' Lantern was not one of the kindly fairies.

So Portlanders had mixed feelings about the pexies. A time came when Christianity had penetrated even to the Island, and the newly converted inhabitants set about building a church (see illustration on following page). They had heard about the troubles elsewhere, and wasted no time in digging foundations which would only excite fairy vengeance. Instead they spent the first day cutting and morticing the timbers for a slender church tower. Before the rising of the evening star, the fabric stood silhouetted against the pale sky, and from its topmost beam a single bell rang out the hour for prayer. The gentle, consecrated sound was torture to the ears of the pexies and before the night was over they had quitted their old haunts for good, streaming in a long procession along the Chesil Beach to search for a new home on the mainland.

Church bells were very important things. Each one had its proper voice, its own name and special powers. Every village was proud of its own bells, and grew very envious if better ones were hung in some

Portland's cliffs and ruins, Church Ope Cove, showing the remains of
both St Andrew's church and Rufus Castle.

neighbouring steeple. It was this envy which lost the great bell of
Knowlton. Today this place is nothing but a farm set among the
empty fields, but in its day the city of Knowlton was the glory of
Cranborne Chase. Seven churches looked down on its busy streets,
and from their towers the bells chimed and boomed to call the
faithful for prayer. Time passed, and undid the works of men. The
streets were empty, and the churches fell into ruin, until at last six of
them were forgotten; only the low earthworks remained, studded
with daisies, to show where churchyard walls had been.

One church was left, and a magnificent bell still hung in its
deserted tower, sounding out a tale of departed greatness. Bellringers
came in from neighbouring villages to admire its sound: at last a
team of three, coming from Sturminster Marshall, got to talking
about the bell, and thinking what a pity it was that such a fine one
should be wasted on a tract of empty countryside when it could be
brought to hang in their own church tower.

The thought soon suggested the crime. They waited prudently until the long nights of winter would conceal them, and then the raid was on. One of the three was sent on ahead with ropes and a saw; squatting high up in the derelict tower, he sawed through the bellframe. From time to time he glanced through the louvred window at the landscape, which was rapidly turning featureless under a fall of snow. Here came a farm cart rumbling towards him over the white fields. Two men jumped off the back: they were his companions, and with trembling care he lowered the great bell down from the tower towards them. Fastening it onto the cart, they whipped the horse and set off on the way they had come, while the snow blotted out their tracks behind them.

Disturbed by the noise, the farmers who lived around Knowlton came to protect their church, but too late. They searched one way and another, unable to find where the thieves had gone, until one of them in despair suggested that they try the arts of an old woman, known to them all as a witch. She flinched as she saw the mob running to her door with torches, but received better treatment than she had feared, and perhaps because of this she agreed to save the honour of the village by revealing, through her art, which way the

The Norman church at Knowlton set in a late Neolithic henge monument.

bell had gone. Galloping horses soon began to gain on the lumbering farm waggon. The Sturminster men listened nervously for sounds behind them, and could not fool themselves that it was only the rising wind, for the shouts and curses of the Knowlton men were all too easy to hear. But in front of them, showing clearer and more distinct through the driving snow, was the familiar tower of Sturminster church. They had only to cross White Mill Bridge and they would be on the other side of the Stour, with their fellow villagers to help them.

They came to the white posts that marked the end of the bridge, but the carthorse shied at the sight of them and the nervous men could not persuade him across. Two of them sprang down and ran across to rouse the village to their help. The third was to stand guard. He paced up and down in the snow, his teeth chattering with cold; his companions could not be seen, and behind him the cries and oaths of Knowlton's defenders rose and fell on the wind, getting closer all the time. At last his nerve failed and he untied the bell, planning to roll it over the bridge and so reach safety. But the snow was slippery under him and halfway across he lost his footing and fell backwards, breaking through the stone parapet with the weight of his burden. Man and bell teetered on the edge for a moment, and then fell with a cry into the sullen river. The pursuers from Knowlton arrived just in time to see a last few bubbles rising to the surface out of White Mill Hole.

They came back later on, weighed down with grapples and pulleys and other lifting gear. Teams of horses, harnessed together, lunged forward at the word of command to pull the great bell out of the river: but all in vain. Often the expectant bystanders would see its massive outline rising dark among the weeds, but then a hook would bend, or a chain snap, and down it sank once more. This was the price of the witch's help – she had found the bell, as promised, and kept it safe from the thieves, but that was all. It would never return to ring out proudly from the church tower, tearing at her black heart with its holy sound, as it had so often done before.

Knowlton was not the only church with an empty space in its belfry. At East Lulworth the tower has space for four bells, but only three are hanging there – the fourth was being brought by sea in a

Two of the eight arches of White Mill Bridge, Sturminster Marshall.

ship which foundered off Arish Mell. In those days the roads were much too rough and treacherous for such a precious cargo as church bells to be entrusted to them, and they were brought in by water instead.

After the parish church had been built at Poole, the traders of the town commissioned a ring of six bells, more perfect in their music than any other peal along the coast. It took a long time to have them tuned and ready to hang, but at last the foundrymaster was ready to dispatch them from the city where they had been cast. Down at the docks he inquired for a ship sailing westwards. There was only one, a little coasting vessel with a grumbling captain who looked on indifferently as the bells were strapped down in the hold. He weighed anchor the next day and set out along the coast, in gradually worsening seas. The captain's temper deteriorated along with the weather, and instead of attending to their duties the crew began to hide in the hold, boasting idly of what they would do with drink and women when they got to Poole waterfront.

Meanwhile the ship was heading for a storm. Lightning cut across the sky ahead, and the waves rose higher, but the sailors took no notice. One of them, looking for an easy place to sit, pulled aside a

A wonderfully atmospheric and exaggerated view of Old Harry rocks.

tarpaulin and discovered the bells. This was something new to the men: they were not regular churchgoers. Trying to puzzle out the Latin inscriptions, they got as far as reading the names of the bells, and that was a source of great amusement to everyone. Then the captain strode in, black as thunder, to ask them what they were up to and why they were not at work.

'Just wondering why bells should have names,' said one pert deckhand.

'Damn the bells!' roared the captain. 'If they really had names, they'd soon tell us about it.'

The treble bell spoke first, chiming out loud and clear, followed by the great bass, and then all the rest of the ring came in on the echo. Their clappers swung wildly to and fro as the ship lurched from side to side, and the waves crashed over the decks. The captain stumbled for the wheel, feeling his vessel twist like a frightened animal under him, while the storm broke overhead. Faster and faster the bells pealed out as the waves tossed the ship back and forth, and the godless crew howled in terror. Then with a cracking, splintering noise she went down in the deep waters just outside Poole Harbour. On winter nights, when the wind is high and the ground swell beats against Old Harry rocks, the sound still echoes on. Fishermen pause to hear the bells beat out their vengeful tune, and listen for the moaning of the crew, who would have prayed for mercy but had never learnt how.

SAXONS AND DANES

Dorset was rich in saints in the early days of the faith. They came from every class, rich and poor, and even kings knew what it was to exchange an earthly crown for the imperishable diadem of heaven. Thus it happened to Edward, son of Edgar the Peaceable, when he went hunting in the royal forest of Corfe. The king had ridden out with his retainers to hunt the deer, but the wild game fled from him across the heather to the shelter of the hills. Every rider raced after them a different way, the king amongst them, until he found himself alone in the forest. The deer had disappeared into the sun-flecked shadows of the wood, and he was lost. Presently, following the hounds, he came to the edge of the trees, and looked up. There he saw a green hill, far away, where the gap of the smooth ridge is cut

An eighteenth century engraving of Corfe Castle.

An icon of St. Edward the Martyr,
who today is venerated at the Orthodox
church at Brookwood in Surrey.

by two jagged valleys. He urged his horse towards it, knowing that near this gap lay the royal hall of Aelfthryth the queen, widow of his father the great Edgar, and mother of his half-brother Ethelred. The orphan king was tired and thirsty, and hoped for a good welcome at the house of his stepmother.

Yes, she was there waiting for him, for she had seen him coming from a long way off and had instructed her servants to give him an appropriate welcome. Now she stood in the shadow of the great hall, a beautiful woman, nobly dressed, holding out a golden cup. Her loyal servants stood to the right and left. Edward the king rode up to her, was greeted by loving words, and took the cup from her hands.

As he lifted it up, the servants clustered close around him. One held onto the reins of his horse, one grasped and twisted his arm, the third slid a long thin dagger through the ribs to his heart. The cup clattered down on the stones: blood mixed with wine flowed mingling down, as the young man gave a great cry and spurred his horse away from the crowd, sinking in the saddle, and then falling. Within the darkness of the hall, the child Ethelred watched wide-eyed at his brother's death. Caught by one foot in the saddle, the lifeless figure was dragged into the woods by its terrified mount, with brambles tearing the body and thorns crowning the face. Quickly the queen's servants ran after it and shook the carcase free before throwing it into the nearby river.

There it lay despised and rejected until, in the dark of evening, unseen hands took it out and placed it in the thatched hut of an old widow who lived by the stream. There was no risk of her identifying the shrouded burden which now shared her cottage, for she had been blind since birth: or so they thought. But that night, when all were asleep, a shining pillar of light shone from heaven, through the gaps in the thatched roof, and came to rest on the body. The old woman raised her head from the rags that served her for bedclothes, and for the first time in her life, she saw light. She hobbled over to the bundle on which it shone and, pulling back the cover, looked down on the young man's face. Realising what had happened, she fell on her knees and thanked God for the making of a new saint.

The queen's men heard of it, and guessing that further miracles could prove embarrassing, they shook the body onto a hastily improvised bier and took it away to Wareham. As they dragged their burden along the dusty road, the old woman kept close behind them, and soon the people of the heath joined in, a ragged procession.

The holy king was buried hurriedly by his enemies, without honour, at Lady St. Mary in Wareham. Before the old woman could limp home that night, masked figures had set fire to her cottage. But it was no use. In the morning, even as a wisp of smoke was still rising from the ashes, water could be seen trickling from the spot. It rose at the point where the pale light of heaven had reached the ground, and it soon widened into a spring, flowing down to meet the river, bearing witness to miracles. The sick came to drink of these waters

Lady St. Mary Church, Wareham, the town's original Saxon minster.

and were healed: the blind bathed their eyes in its flow, and they could see.

Aelfthryth heard of these things, and was afraid. When, a year later, the noble Earl Aelfhere of the Mercians wished to venerate the tomb of the martyr, she was powerless to forbid him, even though it was her own son Ethelred who now wore the tainted crown. The earl had the holy body taken from its ignominious grave and carried in a noble procession to Shaftesbury Abbey, where a shrine was prepared before the high altar. Aelfthryth remained far away in her royal hall, but all around her there was whispering, and at length three from amongst her followers, whom she now shuddered to see, came before her and insisted that she must go and pray before the body of the new saint, for her absence would certainly be taken as a confession of guilt. Quickly she called for the swiftest horse in her stables to be saddled and brought out: but when it saw the pale queen, the horse trembled all over, and would not stir. A second was fetched, but this too rolled its eyes and stood as still as any animal paralysed by a witch's curse. So in the end she had to make the long journey to Shaftesbury on foot: and if that gave her time to think about guilt and suffering and repentance, maybe that too was part of the divine plan.

It is sad when brother turns against brother: but this is the way of kings. Even Edward's great-uncle, the hero Athelstan, had such a stain on his conscience. When he stood ready to be crowned at Winchester, before the sacred ceremony could begin, there was a scuffle as some ruffians tried to seize him and kill him right on the steps of the throne. They themselves were beaten back and bound, and they died that same day, but no-one could find who it was that had put them up to it. As Athelstan sat at the coronation feast, looking over the ranks of his followers, he could not help wondering who had conspired against him. Quietly, the royal cup-bearer called him to one side and whispered an accusation: it was Edwin, the king's brother, who was behind the attack.

This was not true – no-one felt more loyalty for the new king than Edwin – but Athelstan's fear and anger overcame his reason, and he accused his brother of treason. He had too much respect for the rights of the blood royal to put Edwin to death, so he sentenced him to exile instead. But the servants who carried out the king's will had a shrewd idea of what was really intended. They escorted the young prince to a lonely shore, where an old worm-eaten boat was waiting to carry him away. It had neither oars nor rudder. He sat shivering in this craft as they pushed it off: slowly the land drifted out of sight. Then the wind rose, and the waves slapped hard against the rotten timbers, and so Edwin sank and was drowned.

All this time, as his pale body fed the fishes, there was feasting and splendour in the king's hall. The royal cup-bearer was in the thick of it, enjoying the fruits of his work, until his own tongue came to betray him. Strutting about the ale-benches one day, busy with his duties, he happened to slip, but steadied himself by putting one foot in front of the other. 'Well!' he chattered, 'that's how one brother should help another.'

The king heard him and groaned. 'I also had a brother, who might have been my support and stay, and where is he? Drowned in the salt sea, betrayed by the words of wicked men!'

St. Catherine's Chapel, Milton Abbas.

Then Athelstan called for two of his men to strip the finery off the cup-bearer, to bind him tight and do justice on him: and so he died. The king did penance for seven years in expiation of his brother's murder, and founded a house of prayer in the heart of Dorset where priests might intercede day and night for the soul of Edwin. And in this way Milton Abbey came to be built.

Above Milton Abbey, on the slopes of the hill that overlooks the great church where the monks once prayed, there is a little chapel. A soft ascent of grass-grown steps leads up to it, and in the woods that surround it there are faint traces of an abandoned earthwork, originally the embankments around the royal tent when Athelstan marched in war against the heathen Danes. It was a time of trial, when all the enemies of England had banded together, from Anlaf the master of Dublin's pirates, to Constantine the white-haired old king of the Scots. The spearmen of Wessex and Mercia had come to defend the land from them, few against many, and they were camped out on this ridge of hills, waiting until the first glimpse of sunlight would gleam on the weapons of the invaders.

It happened that the place of the king's lodging was known, and that night a surprise attack from a war-party of Danes overwhelmed the sleeping ranks, hoping in the darkness to cut through to where Athelstan lay. He woke with a start, hearing men's cries and the terror of the horses: he threw on his clothes and weapons, and rushed out of the tent to lead his men in the fight. As he ran, he prepared to grip his sword, but horror! in the darkness and confusion, it had dropped out of the scabbard. He was unarmed. Resolving nonetheless to die like a king, he ran to the crest of the hill where all could see him, and called on God and St. Aldhelm to defend the right. Somehow the empty scabbard at his side felt heavier. He reached out, and his hand clutched a sword: he whirled it out and hewed manfully at the backs of the heathen as they screamed and scattered before him.

The dawn rose shining over the Downs, and all that day until the red light of sunset the English drove their enemies westward. When night fell once more, five kings lay dead on the trampled ground, with their ashen-faced followers around them, and the wolves of Marshwood howled at the scent of so much human blood. Athelstan limped wearily back to the abbey church of Milton, and there before the altar he offered up the marvellous sword as a token of the great things that had been done that day.

Many ages went by, but Dorset people did not forget. At length the tales of the old wars dwindled to a hereditary aversion for redheads, who were hissed at as 'Danes' bastards' or, in the more decorous form quoted to policemen, 'red-headed Danes'. This was what they were called at Symondsbury, and also at Wool, where it was explained that in the old days, when there was a king in every county, red-headed men had sailed up the Frome and made terrible ravages on the countryside. They might well be expected to leave a crop of bastards behind them, for no-one could withstand the cruel invaders, man or woman.

At Portland, when the sea-wolves took possession of the place, the streets were deserted. The fire in the smithy was dead, and here and there in the fields a plough stood abandoned in the furrow. The Danes worked their way through the houses, pulling out loot and women, and shouting to each other as they found some poor unfortunate cowering in the bushes. That night they drank and were merry around the fire. A few captives were cut up for entertainment's sake,

The mill pond for Town Mill, surrounded by the stone cottages of Swanage.

and the women were made use of in other ways. At last, when the embers were dying away, each drunken warrior dragged his prize into the nearest house and prepared for bed. The night wore on: a cold moon climbed up the sky, invisible to the snoring invaders. At a pre-arranged signal each woman slipped from her side of the bed, and then, with fire in their eyes and steel in their hands they stabbed and hacked at the sleeping forms with long kitchen knives and cleavers. And their husbands, let loose from the cellars and cupboards where they had lain in hiding, rushed out to finish the work. Never again was the Island troubled by foreigners.

Elsewhere Dorset men made a stand against their enemies. At Swanage, where the survivors of a great sea-fight swam ashore thirsting for revenge, Battle Gate marks the edge of the meadow where they were turned back, just on the northern side of the Town Mill.

At Gillingham the fight swayed up and down the lane that leads to Slaughter Gate, and Slaughter Barrow is the place where the dead of both sides were piled indiscriminately together and given common burial. And at Burton Bradstock the invaders landed on the Freshwater and set off uphill cheerily, expecting easy plunder, with their weapons trailing behind them. They did not know that a silent alarm had been spread, and that further up the road Burton men were waiting grimly under the shadow of the trees. Then there was terrible fighting, for the villagers had determined that not one Dane should return to the shelter of the dragon ships. The battle began just west of Burton Lodge, and the men grappled with each other up and down the neighbouring valley, trampling over the bodies of friend and foe until a sticky mess covered the young grass, and ever since then it has been known as Red Bottom.

KNIGHTS AND PRIESTS

Time would throw more invaders on the Dorset coasts – the French, who landed and sacked the little village of Ringstead, burning down its church while the priest still stood at the altar; the privateers who raided Poole Harbour; the sailors scrambling from the wreck of the Spanish Armada. The stories of these times echo with the sound of fighting. In the church at Glanvilles Wootton lies the tomb of a local knight, Sir Henry de Glanville, whose effigy is shown lying in armour with his feet supported on a lap-dog. He was killed during a skirmish in the forest of Blackmore, defending his lands against some now forgotten enemy. Only after the clash of sword on armour had melted away, and the shouting was over, did the villagers creep through the old trees to search for the body of their lord. They found him stretched out dead under a great oak, with his dog lying lifeless at his feet, and all his enemies vanquished or fled: they carried him back to the church, and buried him still in the same position.

Another memorial effigy, in the chancel of Lady St. Mary church in Wareham, commemorates Sir William d'Estoke, who owned lands along the Piddle and Frome and died in their defence. He was engaged in hand-to-hand combat with the enemy on South Bridge, where today the pleasure-boats are moored and people sit beside the quay gazing across to the Purbeck ridge. It was late summer when the fighting took place, and a swarm of bees came buzzing downriver, looking for a new home. Seeing his massive steel helmet, and taking it for a bee-skep of new and robust design, they settled on poor Sir William and poured in through the crack in his visor. Blinded at a crucial moment in the conflict, his hour of glory was a brief one.

Then again, at Netherbury there is the monument of Sir James More, who was successful in his battle. He had been challenged to a duel, and reluctantly responding to the call of honour he strapped his armour on, came to the field and killed his opponent. As the insolent adversary lay dead at his feet, a white dove settled on Sir James' helmet in token of his innocence and the justice of his quarrel, and this same sign from heaven was remembered many years later when he died, and was carved, just as it had appeared in life, on the crest of his effigy.

There were others who had no time for wars or fighting. Sir John de la Lynde was a hunting man, with kennels at Hermitage and a minute knowledge of the great Forest of Blackmore. His horn had sounded the death-note for every kind of game in these woods, but there was one beast still alive whose pursuit had become a passion with Sir John – the white hart. This stag continued to graze safely in Buckshaw as he had done, time out of mind; his hair had long since turned white out of sheer age, and he bore a head of antlers which the obsessive huntsman longed to see nailed above his own manor house door. But the white hart was too old and too cunning to be caught in the autumn drives of barren hinds. There were stories that he had only been taken once, and that was by the king himself, who had cut the nets and let the proud captive go free. But Sir John did not believe that this could be true.

It was a winter day, and the sun shone low through the branches when the men set out hunting. Sir John rode up towards Holwell, glancing from time to time at the wooded slopes above him, when suddenly there was a cry from the chief huntsman. The white hart had been seen on the hills, and he was a long way from cover. At once the riders tore off after him, with the mastiffs and brachets racing between the horses' hooves. The great beast was running away from the scattered trees, heading for the high ground of the Downs. South of Pulham they lost sight of him, and the dogs had to follow by scent. The track lay uphill; it was hard climbing, the breath of men and horses steamed in the frosty air.

Just below Ansty Cross, in the path they now call Hartfoot Lane, there was a sudden commotion – the hunstmen had come across the track of the stag in the mud, and his slots were facing northwards. He had doubled back on them, and was returning home to the Forest. The hunters turned with renewed vigour, and soon they could see their quarry down in the plain, not as swift in his stride as before, for the long miles were beginning to tell. Sir John knew that the old stag would try to slip unnoticed into the River Lydden to throw off the hounds, so he kept close beside the river.

Cold night was coming on. Only a few riders were left in the chase, though the hounds had kept up. At last the stag made a dash for the river; Sir John whistled the dogs onto him, leapt off his horse and plunged into the Lydden. Wading through the icy water he felt at his belt for the hunting knife and plunged it once, twice into the animal's throat. Blood ran over the white fur and was washed away by the stream. It ran over something bright and shiny – a golden collar, set deep in the folds of fat around the neck. Cut into the gold was an inscription in ancient lettering, which none of the huntsmen could read. They looked at it, and were afraid.

All the stories about the king had been true. Sir John soon found what it was to have killed a royal favourite. He was summoned up to London, bringing the gold collar in evidence, and while he counted the long days in the dungeons of the Tower, learned men puzzled over its writing. At last they annnounced that it came from the days of the Romans, and said that even Julius Caesar had spared the life of the stag – which, of course, made Sir John's offence so much the worse. Liberated from prison on payment of a huge fine, he was deprived of his ancestral arms by the College of Heralds. Instead he was ordered to bear three white stags' heads on a bloody background in memory of what he had done at the ford, which for ever after was known as Kings Stag. A yearly payment, called White Hart Silver, was collected by the Exchequer from the de la Lyndes, and the land over which the great hunt had taken place came to be known as the Forest of White Hart.

It was safer for headstrong knights to travel abroad, confining their feats of valour to foreigners and unbelievers. Geoffrey de Mervin, the young heir to the manor of Stalbridge, made a vow to join the Knights Hospitallers – the order of St. John of Jerusalem. He never saw Jerusalem, a city which had been lost to the infidel long before he was born: instead he found himself penned in among the desperate defenders of the city of Acre, the last bastion of the crusading kingdoms, before it fell to the victorious Saracens. Sir Geoffrey was sent to defend an outpost with the rest of his company, and saw them cut down around him one by one. Felled by a blow from a

Kings Stag, with the now faded image of the White Hart on the old inn sign in the centre of the village.

Muslim sword, he was rescued at the last minute and taken by ship to the Hospitallers' fortress on the island of Rhodes. Here, it was hoped, he might die in peace – for his wounds were infected and all the doctors judged them incurable. That night the pain kept him awake, tossing and turning while his fellows in the long infirmary ward sank into a peaceful sleep. Something caught his eye: there was a light at the end of the room. The light passed down the ward, and he could see that it was carried by a tall man in coarse clothes. His beard was ragged, and his face turned rough by long exposure to the desert sun, but his eyes were full of compassion as he looked anxiously at each sleeping figure. Geoffrey was puzzled. Where had he seen that face before? – and then he remembered the little chapel in the parish church at home, and the statue behind the altar which had first inspired him to take the cross. This was St. John himself, come to minister to his knights. The saint paused by his bedside and pulled out a little bottle of ointment with which he soothed and dressed the young crusader's wounds. Then, in a secret conversation, he told the knight what should be done as a memorial of that night, and after that he moved on into the darkness at the end of the hall.

Early in the morning the doctor and his assistant came through to see who had died in the night. Geoffrey waited motionless until they stood at the foot of his bed, sadly shaking their heads at one another; then he leapt up and clutched the old man in a great bear-hug, ran down the ward and called for his horse and armour. He was healed, without a scar on his body. Relieved of his vows he returned home, married and came to the manor house in Stalbridge, where his first care was to spend a month in the nearest masons' yard commissioning a splendid village cross, with panels to show everything which had happened to him, and an inscription to tell the story. For hundreds of years afterwards, old villagers would linger here to explain to any stranger what the colourful pictures meant, and spell out the old words. Then, all at once, the letters seemed to fade. Deeply carved as they were, they grew fainter overnight and by noon of the next day they had vanished into the body of the stone, which stood as smooth and clear as if it had never been worked. Three weeks later (news carried slowly in those days) the message came that the island of Rhodes had yielded before the overwhelming forces of Suleiman the Magnificent, and that the knights of the order of St. John would go crusading no more.

Not every wayside cross was as elaborate as the monument at Stalbridge. The Cross-in-Hand on Batcombe Down is a stumpy monolith, standing by a track far from any dwelling – but this isolation is itself a witness to the miraculous events which caused it

The Cross-in-Hand, near Batcombe, a wayside cross
perhaps made from a Roman column.

to be erected. Once, on a night of foul weather, the village priest of
Batcombe sat hunched over the fire when he was roused by an urgent
knocking on the door. He opened it, and there was the daughter of
the shepherd who lived up on the Downs. Her father, she said, was
ill, and sinking fast: terrified at the thought of his dying unshriven,
she had come through rain and wind to find someone to give him the
last rites.

Quickly the priest threw on a cloak and hood and ran to the
church where, high above the altar, candles burnt night and day to
mark the place of the Sacrament. He reached for the pyx, the little
silver casket in which the precious burden was stored, and hastily
tied it onto a thong round his neck. Then wrapping his cloak tight
around him, he set out for the crest of the Downs. The wind slapped
and tore at his wet clothing, but he tramped on until he reached a
flimsy hut, and found the dying man where he lay huddled in the
straw. Speaking a few words of comfort, the priest took off his damp

cloak, ready to administer the Sacrament. There was nothing there. Incredulously, he felt round his neck, and touched only the broken thong. Somewhere, out in the pitiless storm, the pyx had been lost.

The old man's eyes saw nothing; they were already distant as the soul drifted away unconfessed, unprepared. He did not hear the slam of the door as the priest ran out, panic-stricken, his heart pounding as he climbed the ridge. Somewhere, out in that dark night, was a little silver box that mattered more than anything else in the world. Looking back along the path, his eyes were startled by a distant light – not a shepherd's lantern or a cottage hearth; much brighter than that. He set out towards it.

The wind shrieked around him, but it grew less fierce as he carried on towards the light. Suddenly, as if he had passed through a curtain, the rain was gone and he stood under a clear sky. From that sky a beam of pure light was shining down, and where it touched the earth he could see, just visible in the ragged grass, a glint of silver. All around it, in a silent watchful circle, were the animals of the Downs; the sheep and cattle, the birds and the shy wild creatures. They were gathered close together, their glittering eyes fixed on the holy presence, only parting to make room for him: then, as he took up the pyx, the light was gone and in the dark he could hear the scampering of feet as they took flight. The storm blew back over him, but the priest did not care. He hurried back to the shepherd's hut where the old man still lingered between life and death; he gave him the viaticum, and waited until all was over. With the morning came an end to the rainy weather, and at dawn the priest retraced his steps slowly and carefully, marking the place of his adventure, and vowing to erect a sign which would tell future ages where the miracle had been.

Every monument tells a story, but they do not always have happy endings. There is a chapel at the edge of the cliffs beyond Worth Matravers – a solid, square building, set just where the land falls away to the sea. Far below, the lonely gulls scream out as they glide effortlessly above the pounding waves. On this point, even before the chapel was built, there had been a lookout; and here a rich merchant stood and watched his ship make her way up the Channel, bound for Swanage. It was a wild day, late in the season. The sea slapped

An engraving of St. Aldhelm's Chapel, built in the twelfth
century as a clifftop seamark.

the rocks and threw up great columns of spray, until beads of wet
dripped off the fur of the rich man's coat: but still he stood at the
edge, watching the ship – not because of the wealth she carried on
board, though all the gold was his and the spices too, but because of
her passenger. It was his only child, and she was coming home for
her wedding. But the ship was well off course, and heading for the
rocks. He watched everything, and did not move. The helmsman
panicked, the inshore waves took hold, the ship shuddered and
lurched. Timbers broke on the sharp rocks that lie under white
water, then bodies were thrown up in the swell. Men struggled
to rescue them, and failed; from above, too far away to help, he
watched them at their work. A merchant must learn to expect loss as
well as gain. Only later, and secretly, did he say something of what he
had seen to a friend who was a master mason – and then it was to
commission the building of a chapel by the cliff. It was to be dedi-
cated to St. Aldhelm the far traveller, and here a priest would pray
for the souls of all those that had perished on the coast. He was to
light a fire, too, on bad nights, to warn the living to keep away from
the rocks: perhaps, also, to give a little light and comfort to the
shivering wraiths of the dead.

CURSES AND CAVALIERS

Generations of worshippers paused to bow to Stalbridge Cross, or kneel within St. Aldhelm's Chapel. None of them could have imagined that these monuments would ever suffer ruin, or that the ceaseless round of intercession and prayer for the dead should fall silent. But it happened nonetheless. In a few turbulent years the Protestant Reformation swept away all the old certainties, beginning with the monastic orders, who had no weapons but spiritual ones with which to defend their lands.

When the King's men came to close down Frampton Priory, the last prior looked closely from face to face and saw nothing there but greed. Each of them was planning how he might acquire this pleasant place, pull down every building that had been set aside for prayer, and turn the rest to vanity. The prior stumbled out, evicted from his home, but before he could reach the gate he was filled with the spirit of prophecy and cried out in a loud voice that whatever was done to turn his sanctuary into a monument of family pride, no eldest son should ever live to inherit it from his father. This came to pass. Frampton Court has never since been handed down from the father to the eldest son.

The common people, too, harboured doubts about the injustices that were done when the church was robbed of her ancient possessions. When Sir Walter Raleigh, still the darling of Elizabeth's court, announced his intention of acquiring Sherborne Castle, old stories became once more the current talk of the town. Osmund, who was the last bishop of Sherborne before the cathedral see moved to Salisbury, had also been a saint. Before his death he uttered a solemn curse on anyone who should rob the Church of her lands in Sherborne, and for three hundred years the anathema had been repeated by each of his successors. During the years of anarchy, when a castle was first built on these lands for safety's sake, King Stephen

A late eighteenth century engraving of Sherborne Old Castle.

came to hear of it, feared that it might be fortified by his enemies, and ordered that it be handed over to him. The Bishop of that time unwillingly complied, and Stephen soon repented of his rash demand. Within a year he had lost his crown and his life, dying without an heir.

The castle passed to the Montague family, and the hands of the curse reached out to them too, for some were killed in battle, others were condemned by the laws and beheaded. At last only one lad was left to inherit the family name. His first tournament was being planned, and his parents were anxious that he should survive the day safely, so they set up a jousting ring at home and took him through the exercises again and again. But a chance blow slipped past his padded shield, and so he died, spitted on his own father's lance. With that the family line came to an end, and the Church reclaimed her own.

So when Raleigh cast a covetous eye on the beautiful fortress, the townsfolk of Sherborne felt it was time to cross themselves. At the very moment that he saw the property, his horse stumbled and fell, and Raleigh fell too, smirching his face and grubbing up the earth

Sir Walter Raleigh (1552-1618).

with his hands. His friends made light of it, saying that it was the beginning of his possession of the land, but others saw it as an omen. Far away in London, the Queen was persuaded to help her favourite, and so she summoned the Bishop of those days and ordered him to alienate the property. He did so reluctantly, knowing well what would follow.

A neglected knife will rust, and poison slowly loses its strength when kept in the bottle – but the edge and venom of a saint's curse stays sharp for ever. Raleigh gained the lease of Sherborne Castle that he had wanted, and he hoped for happiness there, but it slipped through his fingers like sand. First he left England behind to embark on his expedition to Guiana, a costly failure. Soon afterwards, the trial and death of the Earl of Essex, in which he was thought to have had a part, left him the most hated man in the kingdom; and then the old queen died and when James I came to the throne, Raleigh was sent to the Tower, to be executed after years of lonely imprisonment.

He had hoped to leave the tainted lands to his son, but James' eagle-eyed lawyers found a flaw in the document and let them revert to the crown instead. Henry, Prince of Wales, sought a grant of the lands: once in possession of them, he hoped to return them to the Church, but still the work of the curse remorselessly went on, and he died in the flower of his youth, eighteen years old. Possessed once more of the property, James gave it to his favourite Carr, who held it for four years before being attainted for murder. The castle passed from hand to hand, and whoever owned it was sure to meet with disaster.

Soon the work of the Reformation turned from taking property to taking lives, and death could face those who adhered to the old forms of religion. In Elizabeth's reign many Catholic priests were hunted down, like Thomas Pilchard, who was brought to Dorchester to meet his fate. The execution had to be delayed while the

The Venerable Thomas Pilchard, one of the Chideock
Martyrs, hanged, drawn and quartered in Dorchester in
1587 and beatified four hundred years later in 1987.

authorities found someone to perform it, the usual hangman having turned down the job since he was certain that evil luck would pursue those concerned with a priest's death.

Eventually new workmen were found who would set up the gallows, drag the man to it and hang and disembowel him there, as the custom was. They performed their duties and returned home, where shortly afterwards they took to their beds and died, whimpering that they were poisoned by the stench of the priest's entrails.

In his death, Pilchard exercised the spiritual authority which he had been denied while living. The keeper of Dorchester Gaol was going out to water his garden in the cool of the evening, after supervising some small details connected with the execution. He saw a stranger coming down the path, and as the figure came closer recognised him as the man he had just killed. The gaoler asked him what he wanted, and Pilchard said he was sent to visit another prisoner, called Jessopp, who had been his friend while he was alive. 'I shall not be long,' he said as he strode by, 'and presently I shall return for you'. The gaoler sickened during an outbreak of fever, which spread throughout the verminous, overcrowded prison. He told all his visitors how he was set on returning to the old Catholic religion, and when the Anglican vicar tried to offer him consolation, he turned his face to the wall, and so died.

Later on, one of his prisoners – a woman in the last stages of pregnancy – woke in a sudden terror and told her husband that she had dreamt of Pilchard, who told her that it was time to join him. The shock threw her into labour, and this, together with the infected condition of the gaol, proved her death. Jessopp died during the same fever and was buried, as he had requested, near the body of his martyred friend and a few feet away from the gallows.

Three gaunt, grey figures stand today at Gallows Hill, at the end of Dorchester's South Walks. They are statues, by the late Elisabeth Frink, set up to commemorate those put to death at this place for professing their religion, and by extension all who have died 'for Christ and Conscience Sake'. Two of the grey figures represent martyrs, and the third one facing them is Death. On misty nights children hide behind the trees to see if they will get down from their platform and wander around the town.

The memorial by Elisabeth Frink to the Catholic martyrs
in South Walks, Dorchester.

Dorchester folk, by and large, had no time for the old ways. They
embraced the reformed, Puritan religion instead, and as the years
passed they found themselves chafing at the failure of Charles I and
his court to keep up with their own standards of godly zeal. When
things came to a head in the Civil War, the Dorset towns declared for
Parliament, but the county was studded with castles from Sherborne
to Corfe which flew the King's colours, and the country people
found themselves feeding the hungry armies of both sides, with little
enthusiasm for either. In the end the Royalist fortresses capitulated
until there was only one stronghold left – Portland Castle, which
remained loyal after every centre of resistance on the mainland had
given way. The Portlanders would not forget their ancient history –
they were by descent kinsmen of King Ine, the ruler of Wessex in its
glorious days of conquest. He had given them the Island as a secure

The ferry at Smallmouth, Portland's only link with the world before 1839.

possession forever, to be held free of all intrusion by outsiders, and no Portlander had ever acknowledged any master but the King himself.

It was to this stubborn rock that the desperate King Charles fled in his time of trouble. Accompanied only by a small guard, he rode along the coast to Wyke Regis, and paused on the hillside as he contemplated the strength of the Island stretched out before him.

A sound broke in on his reverie. It came from a cottage just off the highway, where a wizened old man was beckoning to him, whispering and flapping the leather apron which he wore – the badge of a smith. 'Your horses, gentlemen! I can shoe them for you, and shoe them well.'

After a moment's hesitation, Charles led his men down into the half-light of the dingy smithy, and there, standing against the red glow of the forge, the old man fitted every horse with a new set of shoes. They were no ordinary shoes, either. For the master farrier had the knack, now lost, of nailing a horseshoe on *backwards*, without any injury to the animal's feet. When the king and his men clattered out from the smithy, they left a trail of prints which pointed deceitfully away from their true track. Now there was no time to lose, and they raced on to Sandsfoot Castle, where the royal banners had once waved – but a glance was enough to show that the Parliamentary ensigns had usurped their place, and so the party turned westwards towards the Chesil ferry, where boats had been made ready to carry them across to the Island.

Meanwhile the Parliamentary garrison, stung into action by the unexpected sound of cavalry, streamed out of Sandsfoot like hounds on a trail. First one, and then another, found the track of hoofprints in the road: and then, misled by the blacksmith's ruse, they raced away in the wrong direction.

On the Island, the brave Portlanders had dug a great ditch around the Verne, and from this makeshift fortress they prepared to sell their lives as dearly as they might. But it was a desperate situation, for they were only simple quarrymen and fishers, with not a soldier amongst them, while soon they knew the full force of the army would be ranged against them on the Weymouth side. At this dark moment it was the women who came to the rescue with a plan, as they had long before in the days of the Danes. They sent all the men down to the foot of the cliffs at Underhill, where they sat in hiding on either side of the road, armed with gads and pickaxes. Meanwhile the women dressed up in their best cloaks, turned them around so that the red lining was on the outside, and paraded stiffly up and down the ramparts of the Verne, broomsticks thrust over their shoulders, saluting at every turn. The trick worked. The enemy, after following the false trail as far as Wyke, turned back to the ferry and looked up at the cliff through the fading light of evening. Their imagination easily populated the fortress opposite with a teeming mass of soldiers, ready to repel every assault, and after a brief agitated conference they decided to retire inland and seek reinforcements. The King was saved.

A good trick is never forgotten. On the slopes of another ancient hillfort, Lamberts Castle in Marshwood, the village girls followed Portland's example and set themselves in battle array with long pikes, the better to frighten off the enemy. And at Lyme Regis women were also putting on red cloaks and men's hats, parading up and down the walls of the town in a show of strength which convinced its besiegers that there was double the expected garrison inside. The difference lay in the politics – Portland had been for the King, while Lyme was staunchly Parliamentary, and had to defend itself against an encircling Royalist force. The townswomen had the last laugh when, after great sufferings, the siege was lifted and the captured Cavaliers discovered just who they had been afraid of.

MONMOUTH AND JEFFREYS

Eventually the wheel of time came full circle: the Commonwealth for which so many Lyme people had given their lives melted away, and the town crier called together all loyal citizens to hear the news of Charles II's restoration. Once more time passed: bells were rung and fires lit for the accession of his Catholic brother James. But the ashes of the bonfires were hardly cold before another proclamation startled the ears of loiterers in the town square.

It was 1685 and late in the evening when a ship came into the Cobb, and a well-dressed young man stepped ashore, followed by an armed guard. He knelt for a moment in prayer on the beach, then bid his soldiers thrust a standard into the wet sand and let its flag unfurl. *Fear Nothing But God*, it said, and the little army shouted out 'A Monmouth! A Monmouth! and the Protestant religion!' It was a cry that would soon echo throughout the West. James, Duke of Monmouth – the illegitimate but Protestant son of Charles II – had come to wrest the kingdom from his Catholic uncle.

Some of those who enlisted at Lyme must have seen action throughout the campaign as far as the walls of Bristol, and so to the end of all hope in the ditches of Sedgemoor. As his fleeing army was cut down around him, Monmouth signalled to his second-in-command, Lord Grey, to follow him: if only they could desert their followers and reach the south coast, it would be easy to bribe a ship to take them to France. But by the time they had reached the long hills of Cranborne Chase, their horses were too tired to carry them any further. Nonchalantly, Monmouth and Grey stopped off at the Woodyates Inn and exchanged their incriminating military clothes for the plain smocks of labouring men. Then they ran down through Horton, looking for somewhere to rest unseen. Here and there in the furzy waste, plots of land had been brought into cultivation: Monmouth saw a field where the beans had grown tall enough to

James, Duke of Monmouth (1649-1685), the illegitimate son of Charles II.

cover a man, and he crept through them, making a bed out of dry fern at the foot of a young ash tree.

There were others on the road too – soldiers, turning over in their heads the bounty they had been offered for taking the fugitives. Two of them came riding down the lane and asked a farmwife the routine question – had she seen a tall stranger, wearing labourer's clothes but fitting them awkwardly? Did he look frightened?

'Yes,' she said, 'that would be the young fellow who stopped at the edge of the field.'

Amy Farrant was the woman's name; her family had farmed in these parts for many years, but were never to do so again. After betraying her master, she never prospered in anything she did, and the whole family sank into poverty until they went on the streets to beg. Then their cottage was left empty, nobody caring to occupy a place with such a reputation. The thatch blew off, the walls got wet and crumbled, and soon nothing remained to mark the spot but tradition.

The capture of the Duke of Monmouth in a ditch beneath
an ash tree near Woodlands.

The Monmouth Ash.

In the beanfield, the soldiers were trudging to and fro, with Henry Parkin their commander in the lead. They were getting nowhere. The sun beat down, and the thought of beer in the Woodyates Inn was very tempting, so they gathered at the edge of the field. A movement caught Henry's eye over by the tree, and he left his men behind for one last look. There, wrapped in a grubby smock, lay the man who would have been King. Henry Parkin wept, and called himself a traitor, though he was supposed to be the most loyal servant of the Crown among them all. But the thing was done.

The other search parties were called off, and Monmouth was sent under guard to London. When one of his captors asked what he would do if set free, the Duke said that, given his own sword and pistol and a fresh horse, he would ride through the army and defy them all to take him again. The reality was different. They took him to Tower Hill and there, after five strokes, an inexperienced executioner succeeded in cutting off his head.

The field where the Duke was taken gained the name of Monmouth Close, and the tree became known as the Monmouth Ash. People came to see it from far and wide, at first out of reverence, later from idle curiosity: just to prove they had been there, they scarred it with their names and dates, an abuse which eventually led to the death of the tree. Its last stump was transformed into some panelling which has been built into the wall of the Monmouth Ash pub in Verwood, and a fresh tree has been planted on the spot as a memorial for future generations.

King Monmouth was not the only one fleeing southward from the shambles of Sedgemoor. Amongst the fugitives was James Daniel from Beaminster – no young hothead off to try his fortune in the wars, but a successful, respected lawyer of the town driven by conviction to place his arms at the service of the new King. Certainly James Daniel could speak with the voice of experience – he was seventy-four. Now for the first time in his life he found himself an outcast, running to the refuge of his home in Hogshill Street. This was no safe place, though, for the soldiers were getting ready to scour the town, looking for everyone known to have supported the uprising. They were led by Colonel Kirke, carried his ensign of a lamb and flag, and were therefore known as Kirke's Lambs. They did not behave like lambs to their victims.

In the night as Daniel lay in bed, he heard a voice from Heaven. Briskly it told him to get up and stop wasting time, to put some clothes on and leave town on the Corscombe road. Hardly had he done so when a cracking, splintering sound showed that the soldiers had broken down the front door, so he left by a back passage, scaled the high garden wall and started to run. He coursed through the fields until he recognised a familiar shape in the moonlight – an old barn that stood isolated in the fields. He had played there as a boy – it was an old family property. Now he crept in and burrowed under the straw. A sleeping hen, who had laid her clutch of eggs in a corner of the barn, woke up and began to cackle: so he grabbed hold of her and pulled her under the straw too.

Meanwhile the troop of soldiers, led by a young lad who had a grudge against Daniel, were looking everywhere in the house and finding nothing. They started to curse the lad for leading them on a wild goose chase, and he, to save his skin, suggested carrying on the search in the old barn at Knowle. They arrived and stood on the threshing floor looking up and down, but it was too dark to see anything. James Daniel heard the voice of the officer ordering two men to guard the door and telling the rest to draw their swords. They were to line up and walk slowly through the barn, stabbing

The burial ground of the Daniel family.

down as they went, listening for the yelp of pain that would tell them they had pricked human flesh and not straw.

Daniel heard the men as they joked and cursed, the rustling of their boots getting nearer, the swish of swords in the straw. In his excitement he let go of the hen, who flew up to the rafters, making the barn echo with indignant noise. There was a pause before the officer called his men off, satisfied that no-one could have entered the barn and left a sleeping hen undisturbed. The soldiers lined up sullenly in the doorway, and went off looking for the lad who had brought them on this fool's errand, and who had now wisely disappeared.

At the first light of morning, James Daniel stole quietly home to his relatives, who kept him secreted in the attic until the time of trouble was over and he could show his face freely in the town again. Then people held him in honour, knowing what he had endured. Daniel, who had seen so much, lived to see a new king and a new queen on the throne, and at last died at the ripe old age of a hundred. There was a curious stipulation in his will – he wanted the old barn at Knowle to be pulled down and its site cleared. There, where God had worked to protect him from evil hands, James Daniel's body was to await the general resurrection. For over ten generations afterwards the Daniels of Beaminster followed the example of their ancestor, until the ruins of the barn had been transformed into a neat little graveyard, with trees and flowers among the headstones.

George Jeffreys (1648-1689), who presided
at the Bloody Assizes of 1685.

Another fugitive was William Bragge, who was heir to the es-
tates of Sadborow, an old manor hidden in the valleys around
Thorncombe. He too returned as a fugitive to his ancestral home,
from which, when Kirke's Lambs began their search, he fled for
refuge over the fields to Higher Laymore farm. It was an old-
fashioned sort of place even then, with a broad fireplace capable of
taking a stack of logs on its hearth, and curing a side of bacon with
their smoke. Some thoughtful tenant had carved out a recess in the
chimneystack where the meat could hang undisturbed. Into this
peaceful household rushed William Bragge, with the soldiers hard at
his heels. As he begged for shelter, the farmer silently pointed up the
chimney, watched as William swung into the hidden recess, and
carried on unhurriedly with the rest of the evening's chores.

Almost at once, the troops tumbled in through the door and began
poking into every corner of the house, while the officer in charge
stood in the hall and rubbed his hands. It was a cold night. Could the
farmer oblige by lighting a fire? He could hardly refuse – and the oak
logs were dry, so it was a fine, warm fire. Bragge stood with his back
to the wall and watched the flames dance up past his face and
clothes. He listened as the surly troopers opened cupboards and

chests and coffers. He heard them leave the house and ride away – then the fire was quenched, and he could come down again, half alive, but free.

But not everyone got away. And those who were captured, and penned together in Dorchester Gaol, could do nothing but wait for the verdicts of Judge Jeffreys in what was to be remembered as the Bloody Assizes. When all the prisoners were gathered together, the Judge rode into the silent county town, where he was to stay at the house in High West Street which is still known today as his lodgings. It is across the street from the church, where he attended divine service on the Sunday before the serious business began. The sermon that week was on the theme of mercy, and it was noticed that this caused the Judge some amusement.

That day he strolled back through the town to his rooms, but afterwards, when the accusing stares of the townsfolk became too much even for Jeffreys' cronies, a secret passageway was opened up from the Antelope, where the trials were held, so that he might come and go unseen. The room set aside for the trials was low, panelled with dark oak, with a table at which the Judge presided at one end,

The panelled 'Oak Room' at the Antelope Hotel, Dorchester, where according to legend the Bloody Assizes were held following the Monmouth Rebellion.

and a dock for the accused at the other. Facing the dock was a little hidden hatch, which the town hangman would open quietly as each new prisoner took their oath, so that he could jot down a rough estimate of height and weight and thus calculate the length of rope they would be needing. Then he cut the rope to size, which would have been wasteful had the accused been found innocent. But Jeffreys never found anyone innocent.

One evening, after a hard day's work and many deaths, the Judge was in his lodgings when a messenger stepped in from outside; it seemed there was a girl waiting in the street who wished to speak with him. He got up and went to speak to her in a separate room. The girl – she was little more than a child – had come to plead for her elder brother, who had joined the Rising as it went north through the town, and had now been led home again in chains. Jeffreys listened stony-faced to the girl's pleas and excuses and then, without changing expression, he made it clear that the young man's life would be granted, but only on a shameless condition. She agreed. They went back into the lodgings, where she shrank from the guffaws of the men and hid in an upstairs room while he finished his evening's business: and so to bed. At dawn the next morning, while the Judge still lay asleep, the girl rose silently and got ready to creep home. Needing more light, she pulled aside the curtains of the bedroom window: and there, on the other side of High West Street, she saw her brother's lifeless body hanging from a peg in the wall.

For a hundred years afterwards, Dorchester women brought their daughters up to spit at the mention of the name of Judge Jeffreys.

As the executions went on, rumour spread among the hopeless country people that God, at least, was on the side of the martyrs. There were twelve men hanged in Lyme Regis alone – they were brought in carts from Dorchester to die in their native town, the place where they had first taken up arms. The gallows was put up on the western shore, on the rough sandy beach where a few months before Monmouth's green standard had been unfurled. Here the carts had to stop just where the road ended, since the beach was too soft to carry wheeled traffic, and a couple of horse-sledges had been commissioned to drag the condemned men for the last few yards to the scaffold.

An engraving of Lyme Regis in 1723, with ships sheltered behind the stone embankment of the Cobb.

That was the plan: but the hand of God intervened. After the twelve prisoners had come off the cart, and were roughly tied down to the sledges, attendants called to the horses to start dragging them over the sand. The horses refused to go. The attendants hit them, whipped them, goaded them, but the horses showed the whites of their eyes and would not stir. So they were unharnessed from the sledges, and fresh horses were put in the traces instead, but with the same result. These new horses would not move when shouted at, and at the first taste of the whip they reared up and broke their harness and the sledges.

At last the twelve prisoners were untied and forced to walk over the sand for their last journey, while the crowd cried shame. Amongst the condemned was Samuel Lake, who had been the Baptist minister at Lyme – he was very old, and would have moved any heart to pity, but among the crowd there was one woman who could feel none for him. When the rope tightened around his neck, she shouted out that it did her eyes good to see such a rebel hanged. Judgement was not long deferred: she lost her sight within a few weeks. Again, there was a man who had sold furze to the authorities, as a useful fuel for burning the entrails after the punishment of disembowelling had been carried out. His real name is forgotten, since he became universally known as 'Burn-Guts' in consequence of this transaction. One by one the horses which he had used for bringing in this freight grew sick and died.

Not everyone concerned in the affair suffered so soon. A lawyer called Jones, who had been very zealous in helping the government, long outlived all the lads whom he had sent to death, and became one of the regular town gentry. His residence at Chatham House was done up in great style, and he grew old in the enjoyment of every pleasure which appeals to persons of taste, with no questions asked about morals. Still, life must end, late or soon: there came a time when notary Jones was on his deathbed. Outside the panes of his sash windows a quick breeze blew up, and clouds were gathering. The old man fell back stiff on the pillow; there was a thunderclap, the gable end of his grand house was torn away by its stroke, and as for his soul. . . . Well, nobody saw anything, but a month or so later a small trading vessel entered Lyme harbour. Her mast was cracked, the sails were torn, but her master had a tale to tell. He had been on the Levantine run from Smyrna, and was making his way back through the straits of Messina when the sun grew pale and darkness covered the sea. Through the murk he could see a ship approaching, lit up by what looked like red lanterns fore and aft. The crew were swarming up and down the rigging – as he got nearer, he could see that they were all devils. Still, sailors must follow the rules of the sea, be they devils or men, so he confidently hailed them and asked where they came from and what was their port. 'Out of Lyme, bound for Mount Etna with Jones!' screamed the devils, and sailed on towards the growling volcano.

FATE AND CRIME

There were many who bound themselves to the Devil, who sold him both their bodies and souls in return for worldly success. It was not a contract to be entered into rashly. Behind a cottage in Powerstock there is a well which supplied the modest needs of the man who lived there alone. He was poor, and no stranger to cold and hunger. On a sharp winter's evening he ran out of water, so he took a candle-stub and lit it to accompany him while he trudged to the well. As the bucket slipped down out of sight into the water, temptation gripped him, sudden as a fever. What if he were to make the infamous bargain? What worlds of wealth and lust and power might open up to him, traded in for his solitary ragged soul? He looked down, and there was the Devil's face reflected in the candlelight. 'Decide!' it snarled.

'Wait!' cried the pauper, 'I must have time! Do wait at least until the candle's burnt out before I decide.'

He clutched at the well-head in an agony of despair, the candle was shaken down into the well, and as it fizzled out in the damp darkness, two hands reached up and pulled the poor wretch down.

None of those who had made the dreadful bargain could expect to get away. A farmer was standing on Eggardon – and the hill at Eggardon is not the sort of place where anyone should go at night, unless they are already friends with the wrong sort – when he heard the sounds of a hunter's horn and the baying of hounds. The quarry soon came in sight – a man, or a man's soul, racing torn and breathless through hedge and ditch. After him paced a tall black fellow who whooped and chivvied on the hounds. He was gaining fast, and caught the fugitive before they got to Askerswell bottom.

The Devil was everywhere. Down French Mill Lane, the track that leads from Shaftesbury to Cann, there was an old barn where the young lads of the village used to meet. Sabbath observance was more strictly enforced in those days, and this was the best place to gather out of sight for a Sunday game of cards. If they heard someone coming, it was easy to scramble quickly under the hay, taking the cards with them as they lay low. On one occasion, however, a stranger was able to slip in and join the party without them noticing it. He was an old gentleman, wearing a dark suit, very polite in his manners. It seemed that he was not at all shocked to see the boys gambling – in fact he rather enjoyed that sort of thing himself – perhaps they would let him join in? They carried on with the game, but it was not so much fun as before. Players were calling out for higher stakes, shouting and swearing if they seemed likely to lose. It looked as if there would be a fight, and some were quietly feeling for their knives. The stranger, who held a winning hand, happened to drop a card, and one of the boys stooped to pick it up for him. He caught sight of one of the black boots. It was very unusual: not shaped for a foot, really, more like a hoof. Standing up and throwing his cards away, he blurted out what he had seen. All was panic. The Sunday gamblers ran headlong to the door, and the old gentleman was left to find his own way back to where he belonged. Shaftesbury was not the only place where this happened. Card-players from Handley and Woodcutts had their secret den in a ruin called the Old Priory, where they were disturbed one Sunday afternoon by a big greyhound which dashed across the room and disappeared. It was a great black dog, with eyes as large as saucers, and no ears. The gamblers were made of sterner stuff than the Shaftesbury boys, and their card games continued on a regular basis, as did the apparition.

It was the poor – ill-fed, dull, aching from labour – who most easily succumbed to the Devil's persuasions. The rich could strike a better bargain, and maybe cheat the old enemy in the end. Wedged in an aisle of Batcombe church is a queer stone monument, half in and half out of the wall – the grave of John Minterne, who had sworn solemnly that his body would never have the refuge of consecrated ground, neither in church nor churchyard. When death came, he equivocated and had himself buried out of the Devil's reach within the church wall.

Conjuror Minterne (which is what people called him behind his back) was a brute of a man, six foot nine in height, and he ruled the

Batcombe's fifteenth century church, between the village and the hillside.

village with a rod of iron. He was suspected of knowing more than he should: there was a secret room in the manor house, where he spent long hours, and no-one else was allowed near it. Once, after watching Minterne ride out of sight on his way to Dorchester, a few of the maids egged each other on to unlock the forbidden door. Clinging to each other and whispering, they entered the room, which was a great disappointment – empty and dusty, with nothing but a lectern in the middle of the floor and an old book resting on it. One of the maids idly turned the cover.

Conjuror Minterne heard the sound. He was a mile away on Batcombe Down, but that didn't make any difference. Turning his black horse around, he rode furiously over the hill until he came to the steep slope where it falls down into the Blackmore Vale. Minterne clapped his heels against the sides of his horse, and it leapt through the air as easy as a bird, over the tower of Batcombe church, and so onto the field at the far side. The horse's hooves burnt the ground where it landed, and grass never grew on that spot again. One of the pinnacles of the church tower, kicked aside by the black creature in its headlong flight, stood crooked ever after, no workman being able to set it back upright. Minterne stormed into the Manor

Lord Milton's house of 1774, its façade overshadowed by Milton Abbey.

and up to the secret room, where the girl was just about to turn the second page. She wheeled around at the sound of footsteps, and there was her master in the doorway, handing her notice of dismissal. If she had succeeded in turning the page, maybe she would have seen something worse.

But the rich are also subject to fate, as the people of Milton Abbas found out. Once this was a busy little town, nestling up against the grey tower of the Abbey, with the mansion house built on the other side where the monks had been dispossessed. In the town there was a school, and in the school there were boys who, like boys everywhere, were fond of fruit and thought stolen fruit was the sweetest. The mansion of Lord Milton had elegant terraces and a classical façade but, most important for the boys, it had an extensive orchard round the back of the kitchen garden. Every autumn, they found a way in somehow and swarmed over the apple trees. Lord Milton decided that enough was enough. He solved the problem satisfactorily – from his point of view – by pulling down every house in the town, building a new village for the tenants away from his sight, and drowning as much of the old village as he could under the waters of an artificial lake.

Worse was to come, for in his hurry to surround the big house with sweeping lawns, Lord Milton had given orders to level the site of the old churchyard. Generations had been buried there, a hump in the grass their only memorial, but what was that to him? The gardener's men set to reluctantly until they came to disinter the first old burial; then they looked at each other in silence, and all downed tools. Their employer, glancing out of the window, saw them and was furious. He stormed out into the grounds, where the men stood stubbornly at the edge of their trench, with a few mute bones perched above it.

Ignoring the living, Lord Milton harangued the dead. 'What! Are my men to be put off working by a lousy skull!' – and he booted the offending relic into a corner of the field, drove his labourers back to work, and returned to his papers.

At last the work was done, and the great house stood, as it stands today, alone amongst the level greensward. But Lord Milton did not enjoy his solitude for long. Something started to tickle him, though it was not reproach: something started to bite him, but it was not conscience. He got no rest, night or day. From their regimented new village, Milton people saw how sheets and linen were being washed each day, and how a string of doctors came to call at the big house. Time came when the truth could no longer be kept silent – Lord Milton was being eaten up by lice. His brutal words to the skull had been returned with interest, and the vermin continued to gnaw at him until life itself was a burden. He died, and was buried in the abbey under an effigy of deceptively serene white marble.

Fate, which had intervened so decisively to punish the guilty, was just as quick to protect the innocent. In the same church, only a few yards from where Lord Milton's infested body was laid to rest, young John Tregonwell had played as a toddler, clambering earnestly up the stone steps, and venturing one day to run to and fro on the battlements. His parents, discovering him perched on these dizzy heights, let out a scream of terror – the next moment he had lost his footing and was plummeting downwards. But a kindly Providence saw to it that, in the fall, his long babyclothes billowed out around him. They acted as a sort of parachute, and he came safely to ground.

The same fortunate intervention saved a girl from Portland who, having been crossed in love, took herself to the cliffs at Weston determined on suicide. The moment that she threw herself into the giddy air, however, her hooped skirts spread out and she landed on the beach not much the worse for wear, changed her mind about dying, and got herself another lad for her husband.

Not that it is ever wise to tempt Fate. Once, a man from Wimborne was convicted of an offence which, under the savage legal code of that time, carried the sentence of death. Not long before this, there had been a dispute among the town elders about the danger of allowing free access to the central tower of Wimborne Minster: surely if anyone were to fall from that height, the results must be instantly fatal. Now the unfortunate prisoner was called into the town chamber and given a stark choice – he could be hanged there and then if he liked, but the alternative was to hurl himself off the tower, as a kind of living experiment.

It didn't seem much of a choice, but he grasped at his only chance and warily ascended the tower, throwing himself headlong . . . and landing on his feet down below, miraculously unhurt. People clustered around him. Did he have a charmed life? How he could have done such a thing? 'It's easy, really', he said, shrugging his shoulders and looking at the girls. Then he sprinted back up the turret steps to repeat his performance, waved from amongst the pinnacles, jumped a second time, and broke his neck.

If a man really is destined to be hanged, there is no chance of him getting away from it. Amongst the savage old laws was that against sheep-stealing – it was death to be caught in possession of an animal, but some men, driven by daring or hunger, would pilfer a live supper if they could. A fellow from Batcombe had long made this his secret trade, slipping out in the twilight to view the flocks as they stood in their folds among some hollow of the downs. He was at this one foggy night, and passing unobserved over other men's land he made his choice of a fat ewe, trussed her up with all four legs tied together, and slung the body over his back.

Then it was time to turn homewards, to kill and hide his prize before other folk were about. Humping the stolen weight up onto the ridgeway was hard work, and he felt the need of a respite, so he was glad when he saw the dark stump of the Cross-in-Hand looming ahead of him out of the mist. He heaved the sheep up on top of the stone, and leaned gratefully against it for a rest. As his eyes

Wimborne Minster from the River Stour in the eighteenth century.

closed drowsily for a moment, the sheep began to struggle, dropping down on the far side of the stone: frantically she pulled at the rope which the man had passed round his neck, stretching it tighter and tighter. Later, in the first hours of daylight, an early traveller on the road came across the luckless thief still lying there, strangled by his bleating victim.

Hanging was normally a more public business than this, with the whole town turning out to escort the luckless convict to his last drop. When so many crimes were punished by death, executions became quite a regular affair; at Dorchester a cottage had to be set aside for the hangman, in a pleasant spot outside the town and beside the clear waters of the Frome. From here the official would bustle through the town to the shire court, where he could meet up with the sheriff's officers and be introduced to his forthcoming victim. The party would then proceed down High East Street and stop off at the Old Bell for a drink before the more unpleasant part of the affair commenced. There was one criminal who would have none of this,

Hangmans' Cottage, Dorchester, in a tranquil spot by the River Frome.

even though the drink was already paid for, and he insisted that the whole horrible business be got over and done with. Reluctantly the hangman and his mates gave in, left their beer untouched in the snuggery, and left for work at Gallows Hill. Just as the grim job was finished, they saw a frantic figure racing down the road towards them, with a sheet of paper in his outstretched hand. It was a messenger boy with a pardon for the prisoner, which might easily have reached him had he been sipping that last valedictory pint.

There were worse fates than hanging, as the murderers of Thomas Baker were to discover. Baker was expected back from Dorchester market by his wife and children, with pockets full of gold from an honest day's trading. But evening grew into night, and they hung up lanterns by the farm gate down in Melbury Bubb; still there was no sound, until the clatter of hooves was heard on the road and Baker's horse tore wild-eyed into the yard, riderless, the saddle hanging loose and speckled with blood. Grabbing the lanterns, they raced up the road until they came to a pit by the old Dorchester road, and there at the bottom of it lay Baker's body, his head smashed in by a blow from a jagged stone.

Nobody could find who was responsible, and the family were close to despair – but murder will out. Seven years had passed, and the son of the family had grown into a man, working the farm in the day and sometimes off to the Acorn Inn in Evershot for a drink in the evening. The usual crowd were there, including two shabby types from the end of the village who seemed a bit worse for wear that night. Young Baker kept his distance from the pair as they spat abuse at each other – liar, pickpocket, cut-throat. . . Now he was really listening to their vicious mumblings.

'Call me that, would you?' said one. 'It was you that pushed old Baker off his horse.'

'So maybe it was, but who threw the great stone on him as he lay on the ground?' said the other.

The young man got up and had a quiet word with the landlord, while the two drunks carried on hissing and hiccuping at each other until they rose unsteadily to go home. Then they found the doors barred, and every man in the place standing round waiting for them, with faces set like iron.

The men were convicted at Dorchester assizes and sentenced, not to be hanged there and then, but to be punished at the place of their crime. Two cages were taken from the gibbets where, after the usual custom, they had held dead men's bodies; each of the murderers was clamped alive into one, and hoisted from a branch of the tree that hung over the pit. And there they stayed, screaming and flailing their hands through the bars as travellers coolly passed by on the Dorchester-Sherborne road. Only one person responded to their cries for help. She was a stranger, down from Yeovil for the day with a few goods for sale: she had no food on her but, pitying the men and knowing nothing of what they had done, she took out two tallow candles and thrust one into each of their mouths. The law is not so easily despised, however, and for her act of charity she served seven years' imprisonment in Dorchester gaol.

Still, familiarity breeds contempt, and men would play practical jokes even in the presence of the dead. There were three brothers who had settled down for the night in a Dorchester pub, while the wind howled in the chimney and the last leaves of autumn danced against the windows. 'It's a cold night,' said the landlord, 'especially for such as dance outdoors'. He was referring to the criminal who had been hanged that morning, and was swaying in the wind from the gallows a mile away at Monkeys Jump.

Idly the men sank their beers, each one boasting of his fearlessness in the face of the unknown, until the two older ones put the youngest to the test. Would he go out alone to the place where the hanged man was swinging, and offer him – poor cold soul – a bowl of soup to keep him warm that night? Well, there was no backing out of it for the youngest: he had to agree, and the grinning landlord fetched a steaming bowl of broth from the kitchen. Out he went, whistling uncertainly to himself – then the eldest leaned across the settle and whispered out a plan to his brother.

While the young lad marched uneasily up High West Street with the soup, the other two raced down lanes and across gardens, not pausing until they had arrived first at the gallows. They lay down behind a wall to catch their breath, and it was not long until they heard footsteps as the lad came nearer. He saw nothing ahead of him but the gallows, with the corpse staring down at him. Mechanically, determined to win his bet, he held up the soup to the dead man.

At that moment one of the others roared out, 'Blow it, it's too hot!' and leapt up from the place of concealment. The poor lad dropped the bowl. Soup splashed on the grass as he fled screaming across the dark fields, away from the clammy horrors of legend, and back to the comforting lights and warm fires of home.

FURTHER READING

Dorsetshire Folklore by John Symonds Udal (1922, reprinted in 1970) is still the only comprehensive study of the subject. Udal collected his material, mostly from written sources, from the 1880s onwards; unlike many of the Victorian folklorists he is not given to fanciful interpretations. Folklore was often used by Thomas Hardy, and two writers who knew the novelist and his background bring together these references – Wilkinson Sherren in *The Wessex of Romance* (1902) and Hermann Lea in *Thomas Hardy's Wessex* (1913). Hardy gave his own sardonic spin to tradition – for a truer idea of what Dorset people thought and felt, read the poetry of William Barnes. A selection has been edited by the Dovecote Press (1984). Marianne Dacombe published a mass of local tradition gathered from Women's Institutes as *Dorset Up Along and Down Along* (1935). More recently, Kingsley Palmer has written *Oral Folk-Tales of Wessex* (1973), which covers Somerset as well as Dorset. He is careful to transcribe what people said to him, rather than to retell the stories. Edward Waring also presents his material as a folklorist in *Ghosts and Legends of the Dorset Countryside* (1977) – he gives short notes on all the different versions of a tale, including those in obscure early sources. Rodney Legg, who has been interested in Dorset folklore for many years, includes legends and anecdotes in *Mysterious Dorset* (1987). I have put together what is known of the folklore of ancient monuments in the country as *Cuckoo Pounds and Singing Barrows* (1986), and the Giant now has his own book, Rodney Castleden's *The Cerne Giant* (1996).

ACKNOWLEDGEMENTS

Most of the illustrations in this book are from the Dovecote Press Collection but I am grateful to the following for allowing the inclusion of illustrations in their possession or for which they hold the copyright. Front cover illustration: by permission of The British Library (*Sherborne Missal*), manuscript reference number ADD MS 74236 (formerly loan 82, page 489). Cambridge University Collection of Air Photographs: page 25. Roger Holman: back cover, page 17. Francesca Radcliffe: frontispiece. Royal Commission Historical Monuments (England), © Crown Copyright: page 36. The Saint Edward Brotherhood, Brookwood, Surrey: page 34.

The

DISCOVER DORSET

Series of Books

A series of paperback books providing informative illustrated
introductions to Dorset's history, culture and way of life.
The following titles have so far been published.

BRIDGES *David McFetrich and Jo Parsons*

CASTLES AND FORTS *Colin Pomeroy*

CRANBORNE CHASE *Desmond Hawkins*

GEOLOGY *Paul Ensom*

THE GEORGIANS *Jo Draper*

THE INDUSTRIAL PAST *Peter Stanier*

ISLE OF PURBECK *Paul Hyland*

LEGENDS *Jeremy Harte*

PORTLAND *Stuart Morris*

POTTERY *Penny Copland-Griffiths*

THE PREHISTORIC AGE *Bill Putnam*

SAXONS AND VIKINGS *David Hinton*

SHIPWRECKS *Maureen Attwooll*

STONE QUARRYING *Jo Thomas*

THE VICTORIANS *Jude James*

All the books about Dorset published by The Dovecote Press
are available in bookshops throughout the county,
or in case of difficulty direct from the publishers.
The Dovecote Press Ltd, Stanbridge,
Wimborne, Dorset BH21 4JD
Tel: 01258 840549.